Meerkat

by Grace Hansen

abdopublishing.com

Published by Abdo Kids, a division of ABDO, P.O. Box 398166, Minneapolis, Minnesota 55439.

Printed in China

102017

012018

Photo Credits: iStock, Shutterstock

Production Contributors: Teddy Borth, Jennie Forsberg, Grace Hansen

Design Contributors: Dorothy Toth, Laura Mitchell

Publisher's Cataloging in Publication Data

Names: Hansen, Grace, author.

Title: Meerkat / by Grace Hansen.

Description: Minneapolis, Minnesota : Abdo Kids, 2018. | Series: African animals |
Includes glossary, index and online resource (page 24).

Identifiers: LCCN 2017943136 | ISBN 9781532104206 (lib.bdg.) | ISBN 9781532105326 (ebook) |
ISBN 9781532105883 (Read-to-me ebook)

Subjects: LCSH: Meerkats--Juvenile literature. | Mongooses--Juvenile literature. |
Zoology--Africa--Juvenile literature.

Classification: DDC 599.74 --dc23

LC record available at https://lccn.loc.gov/2017943136

Table of Contents

Meerkat Habitat

Meerkats live in Africa. They are found in deserts and grasslands near Africa's southern tip.

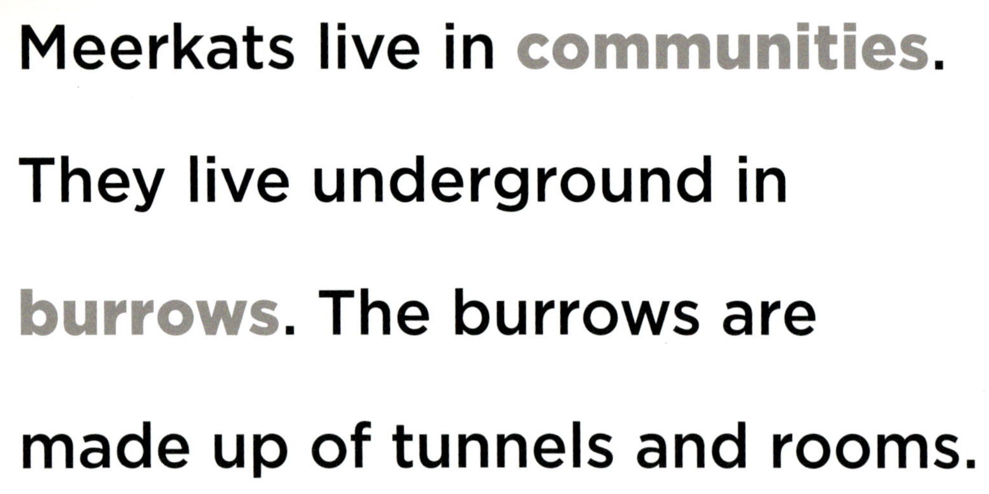

Meerkats live in **communities**. They live underground in **burrows**. The burrows are made up of tunnels and rooms.

Burrows keep meerkats both cool and safe. **Predators**, like birds, cannot snatch them when they are underground.

Body

Meerkats are covered in light brown fur. They have stripes on their backs.

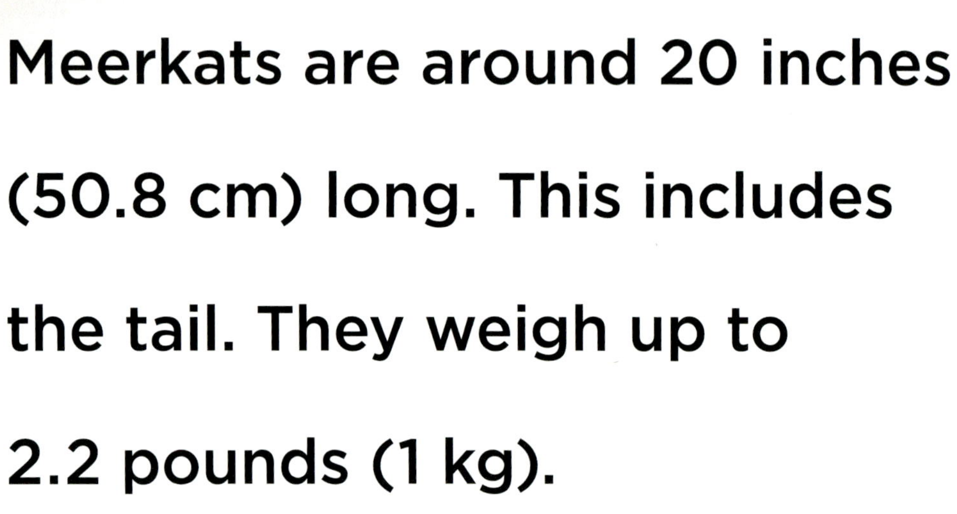

Meerkats are around 20 inches (50.8 cm) long. This includes the tail. They weigh up to 2.2 pounds (1 kg).

Meerkats move on all four legs. They often stand upright to watch for **predators**.

Food & Hunting

Meerkats are good hunters. They mostly eat insects, which they can easily find. They also eat small **rodents** and reptiles.

Baby Meerkats

Females give birth to 2 to 4 babies. Baby meerkats are called pups. Pups are very small. They are kept safe in the **burrow**.

At 4 weeks old, pups leave the **burrow** for the first time. The group helps raise the pups. It teaches the pups how to hunt, be safe, and play!

More Facts

- Meerkats have long, sharp claws. They use their claws to dig **burrows** and dig for prey.

- Females are often larger and stronger than males. Females lead the **community**. Each community has about 40 to 50 meerkats.

- Meerkats work together to stay safe. One meerkat is made to be the lookout. It finds a high area to watch for **predators**. If it sees a predator, it will make a loud noise. This warns the others to hide.

Glossary

burrow – a hole or tunnel dug by a small animal.

community – a group of the same animals living together.

predator – an animal that hunts and eats other animals.

rodent – a small, nibbling animal that has two large front teeth.

Index

Visit **abdokids.com** and use this code to access crafts, games, videos, and more!